And so to Bed

MARGARET WILLES

The National Trust

FOR VICTOR

First published in Great Britain in 1998 by
National Trust Enterprises Ltd
36 Queen Anne's Gate, London SW1H 9AS
http://www.ukindex.co.uk/nationaltrust/bookshelf

British Library Cataloguing in Publication Data
A catalogue record for this book is available from the British Library.

ISBN 0 7078 0279 2

ACKNOWLEDGEMENTS

p.3: Quotation taken from the book *Alias Grace* by Margaret Atwood published by
Bloomsbury Publishing Plc in 1996. Reprinted with permission of the author and Curtis Brown Ltd.
Inside back cover: Diagram of a seventeenth-century bed drawn by Peter Thornton is taken from his book
Seventeenth-Century Interior Decoration in England, France & Holland published by Yale University Press in 1978.
Reproduced by kind permission of the author and the publishers.

Picture research by Margaret Willes
Designed and typeset by Peter and Alison Guy
Production by Dee Maple
Print managed by Centurion Press Ltd (HGP)

Front cover: Peg Woffington, one of the leading actresses of eighteenth-century England. The unknown artist has shown her in bed, after she was struck down by palsy on stage in 1757. This portrait hangs in Beningbrough Hall, Yorkshire.

Title page: The middle aged lady in the double bedded room, illustration from The Pickwick Papers by Charles Dickens (1874 edition).

Back cover: Detail of one of the gilded hawk's heads on the headboard of the early eighteenth-century state bed at Erddig, North Wales.

Introduction

When I embarked on this project, I thought I knew exactly what a bed was, and how it developed over time. But the more I delved, the more complex the subject became. First of all there was the language. *Call my Bluff* would have a wonderful time with sparver, dornix and bere – all to be found on the following pages. Second, there was the question of the state bed. I have been admiring state beds for years without asking why they existed and who slept in them. I am grateful to Annabel Westman, who has tried to navigate me through the tricky layers of the state bed. The Trust owns a lot of these: I have mentioned as many as possible, but there are more out there to explore and enjoy.

This book is organised in a roughly chronological order, from the Middle Ages to Modernism at Willow Road. I have taken Samuel Pepys' famous line for the title as I talk not only of beds, but of bedchambers, their furnishings, how they were heated, lit and cleaned, and of their ancillary rooms – the closet, dressing room and 'little room' – not coyness, but how Bess of Hardwick's lavatory was referred to in her inventory.

Beds take on a quite alarming significance when one realises that the state bed represented the monarch or nobleman, and thus was not to be bounced upon lightly. For an ordinary household, the bed represented the most expensive item apart from the house itself – the medieval or Stuart equivalent of a car or a yacht. And, of course, it marked the phases in one's life. As Grace pointed out to Dr Jordan in Margaret Atwood's *Alias Grace*:

> … you may think a bed is a peaceful thing, Sir, and to you it may mean rest and comfort and a good night's sleep. But it isn't so for everyone, and there are many dangerous things that may take place in a bed. It is where we were born, and that is our first peril in life; and it is where the women give birth, which is often their last. And it is where the act takes place between men and women that I will not mention to you, Sir, but I suppose you know what it is; and some call it love, and others despair… And finally beds are what we sleep in, and where we dream, and often where we die.

So, I finish the text with the marriage bed, the childbed, beds for children and the deathbed.

I have received a lot of help from my colleagues at the National Trust, but I would like particularly to thank Oliver Garnett for his indefatigable provision of texts and references.

When William Shakespeare bequeathed his 'second best bed with the furniture' to his wife, Anne Hathaway, he intended her no marital slight. In medieval and Tudor times a bed was the most valuable possession in a household, and featured prominently in the assignment of property. The Earl of Arundel even gave his bed a pet name, Clovis, while it was customary for the monarch to take the beds of disgraced nobles who had forfeited their estates. Shakespeare quite properly left his best bed to his daughter and heir, Susanna.

Beds of this period were usually box-shaped, with rope stretchers for holding boards on which the mattress could lie. These stretchers had to be tightened regularly – hence the expression sleep tight. The structure of the bedstead did not make it easy to move, so it usually stayed in the chamber, while the bed furniture – hangings, linen, mattresses, pillows – could be transported: a vital factor for wealthy households, where the lord and his servants moved from one residence to another.

The Percy Earls of Northumberland, for instance, owned twenty residences in England, including Petworth in Sussex. Household ordinances, compiled for the 5th Earl in 1512, were intended to keep the show on the road. Two carriages were required to transport the beds of the chapel household: the Dean, sub-Dean, priests and children of the Chapel, and the Groom of the Vestry. Adults were expected to sleep two to a bed; children three.

Only the richest and most elevated in the land enjoyed their own bed. Even they would have shared their bedchamber with servants, who slept on straw pallets on the floor, or in a truckle, a bed on wheels that was stored under the main bed during the day. To provide some kind of privacy, curtains were hung from a sparver (from *epervier*, the French for sparrow hawk), a canopy suspended from hooks on the ceiling. In time the canopy became part of the structure of the bedstead, as in the four poster, with the curtains hanging from the tester. The ingenuity of the upholsterer was invoked to cover as much of the woodwork as possible with fabrics.

Descriptions of medieval bedchambers suggest that they were sparsely furnished, with a chair, a coffer at the foot of the bed for clothes and other belongings, and an aumbry, a cupboard in which food could be kept, for breakfast was usually eaten in one's chamber. The chair was often X-shaped and jointed so that it could be folded up and carried, like the bed furniture. Early seventeenth-century examples of this type of chair, upholstered and with cushions, can be seen at Knole in Kent.

The idea that the bed and its furnishings represented the status of the owner can be seen at Hardwick Hall in Derbyshire, built in the 1590s by Elizabeth Talbot, Countess of Shrewsbury, better known as Bess of Hardwick. By marrying and burying four husbands, Bess had become one of the richest women in England. The actual construction of the New Hall at Hardwick cost her about £5,000, but she spent considerably more than this on the magnificent furnishings.

It was becoming much more the norm for wealthy families and their upper servants to have their own bedchambers. Bess, at the top of the social ladder, had a whole suite of private apartments on the first floor. Her bedchamber has been altered, but an inventory taken in 1601 shows that this room was hung with tapestries. The posts of the bedstead were covered with scarlet, 'laid on with silver lace', while the valance was also of fine scarlet cloth trimmed with gold braid and fringe.

None of Bess's many beds survives, but in the Blue Room can be seen the bed belonging to Christian Bruce, who married William Cavendish, 2nd Earl of Devonshire and presided over Hardwick less than 20 years after Bess's death. The blue damask hangings that almost hide the wooden bedstead were not surprisingly beyond repair by the nineteenth century so had to be replaced, but the gold embroidery is original. The decorative scheme is carried through to the *en suite* chairs.

Although there was only one chair in Bess's Bedchamber at Hardwick in 1601, it had a rich covering of russet satin striped with silver, and was supplemented by stools. Other contents included velvet-covered books, an hour glass, cupboards, a looking glass, hairbrushes, three leather-covered desks, a writing-desk, and a series of coffers, boxes and trunks. There was a bedstead for Bess's grand-daughter, the Lady Arabella, with a canopy of blue and white dornix, a mixture of linen and wool, and a pallet with its own mattress and bolster. Leading off this crowded room was a 'little room' which housed Bess's chamber pot or close stool, discreetly placed in a box covered in blue cloth stitched with white, red and blue silk fringe.

Bess's rooms were furnished in the most lavish way – furniture matching the decoration of the bed, for instance, was a rare luxury. The bedchamber of one of her upper servants, Mr Reason, in the Old Hall at Hardwick is more typical of most moderate Tudor households: a wooden bedstead with a tester and turned posts, two blankets, two coverlets, a square table, a carpet of green cloth, a chair and a joint stool.

Of down of pure dove's white
 I will give him a feather bed
Rayed [striped] with gold and right well cled [covered]
 in fine black satin doutremer [from overseas]
And many a pillow and every bere [pillowcase]
 of Cloth of Rennes to sleep soft.

A fisherman with his dog and birds, a detail of appliqué embroidery from one of the sixteenth-century bed valances belonging to Bess of Hardwick. The embroidery would have been applied to a background of plain velvet.

These lines come from *The Book of the Duchess*, Geoffrey Chaucer's earliest poem, probably written in 1369 as a memorial to Blanche, Duchess of Lancaster, who had died the previous year. Chaucer was familiar with bed furnishings, for he served as a Valet of the Bedchamber to Blanche's father-in-law, Edward III.

The finest mattresses were wool sacks stuffed with down and feathers, although Leonardo da Vinci was outraged that people should want to 'lie as though dead upon the spoils of other dead creatures'. Substitutes for feathers included straw, gorse, and even seaweed; the mattress of the State Bed in the Venetian Ambassador's Room at Knole (p.16) was recently discovered to be filled with lawyers' wigs. For Bess of Hardwick, however, only feathers would do, in sacks of ticking, which would be passed to the servants when they were worn out.

Bess's other furnishings reflected Chaucer's *doutremer*, with silks for her hangings, valances and coverlets imported from Italy, Spain and the Near East, and linen for sheets and pillowcases from the Low Countries. The Hardwick accounts list a bewildering series of materials, the names of which are often derived from the towns where they were made: dornix, a linen and wool mixture, came from Dornix or Tournai; fustian, cotton with a linen warp used for the best blankets, came from Fustat in Egypt, though by the sixteenth century the best blankets came from Spain and cheaper fustians were being made in Lancashire; damask, the rich silk for hangings, came from Damascus. Not all are from overseas, however: kersey, a woollen cloth, comes from a village of the same name in Suffolk.

Bess's household was large, and the inventories reflect this: 250 blankets, 170 fledges (p.24), fustians and rugs, 250 coverlets and quilts were listed in 1601. Most of these bed furnishings have disappeared, but remarkably some survive. One such is a coverlet made in Bengal, with a thick layer of wadding sandwiched between layers of white cotton, and decoration provided by backstitch embroidery of red, blue, green and orange silk worked through the layers. Bess's son William Cavendish was involved with the East India Company, founded in 1600, which may explain how this rare piece came to be at Hardwick.

The High Great Chamber, one of the magnificent state apartments on the top floor at Hardwick, where Bess would receive her honoured guests. This detail shows the canopy of state in purple velvet, decorated with appliqué embroidery, and the chairs of state raised on a dais covered with a carpet.

The idea of the state bed seems to have come from medieval France and the *lit de justice*. The bed would be placed wherever the kings who held the holy crown of France might sit in judgement. This concept was reflected in the sixteenth-century Tudor court, where Henry VIII's furniture of estate or state was his bed; his throne, the seat of authority; and his buffet or cupboard for the display of plate. Household regulations warned that anybody, whatever their rank, must not approach the king's throne under its cloth of estate, nor lean upon the king's bed, nor approach the cupboard. An inventory taken at Henry's death in 1547 described his bed at Hampton Court as having a carved, painted and gilded bedstead with sumptuous hangings of cloth of silver and gold, and curtains of white and purple taffeta.

This bed of estate was not for sleeping: it stood in the formal, state apartments and was used for the daily ritual of going to bed in the evening and rising in the morning. Henry VIII actually slept in smaller, more comfortable beds in bedrooms elsewhere – at both Hampton Court and Greenwich, he had two bedchambers in his own lodgings and a third in the Queen's lodgings.

Bess of Hardwick was much at court in the 1540s, when she was married to Sir William Cavendish, so was familiar with this arrangement, and like other courtiers, reflected it in her own house. Her state apartments at Hardwick were on the top floor, with a long gallery stretching the full length of the house, alongside a High Great Chamber, where Bess would dine with her favoured guests, through the Withdrawing Room, where guests would withdraw for entertainment after dinner, to the Best Bedchamber. Here Bess erected the magnificent bed made for her marriage in 1547 to her second husband, Sir William Cavendish. This had 'a double valance of black velvet embossed with cloth of gold and cloth of silver embroidered with gold and pearl with curtains of yellow and white damask'.

Bess planned the sequence of state rooms partly to emphasise her social standing, partly in the hope that Queen Elizabeth might one day pay her a royal visit, and partly as an appropriate setting for her grand-daughter Arabella, who had a claim to the English Crown. The apartments are still magnificent and breathtaking in their scale, but naturally somewhat faded. In the High Great Chamber, the visitor can look upon the canopy of state installed at a later date, with its chairs and flanking stools, and get some idea of the brilliant colours of the original hangings – purples, yellows, cloth of carnation, tawney and murrey, some of which we would find clashing. But to Bess's guests, as they wandered through the rooms admiring the tapestries and appliqué hangings of the personifications of the Virtues and Vices, the effect of the flickering candles and firelight on the tissue of silver lace and cloth of gold must have been magical.

Although Charles II never adopted the very elaborate rituals of his cousin, Louis XIV of France, who made getting up and going to bed a form of theatre, he stipulated that access to his state bedchamber should be enjoyed only by princes of the blood and specific household officers. The French fashion, adopted by the Stuarts, was to have the state bed in an alcove, with a balustrade separating it from the rest of the room. At Powis Castle in North Wales, the state bedroom still carries this arrangement, the only one to survive in Britain. It was probably prepared for the visit in 1684 of the Duke of Beaufort as Lord President of the Council, and therefore the King's representative in Wales.

At Hampton Court Henry VIII's apartments were swept away in the 1690s and new ones designed for William III by Sir Christopher Wren. These followed the principle of moving from the public guardchamber through a series of rooms, including the Presence and Privy Chambers with thrones under canopies of state, to the State Bedchamber with the state bed. Privilege of access marched with this progress. An account of the visit of the King of Spain and Prince George of Denmark, consort to Queen Anne, to the 'Proud' Duke of Somerset at Petworth in 1703 shows how the niceties of hierarchy could take on the style of an elaborate gavotte. First, the King received the Prince in his bedchamber by advancing to the door and then, sitting in the X-shaped chair of estate at the foot of his bed, invited his guest to a chair opposite. When the visit was reciprocated, the Prince, being of lower rank, came to the door of his apartment to welcome his guest before leading him back through a withdrawing room and ante room to his bedchamber.

A late echo of this hierarchy and symbolism is to be found at Blickling Hall in Norfolk. The state bedroom was redecorated in the 1770s in the fashionable neo-classical style, but the bed was placed behind a screen of columns in the fashion of the Stuart alcove chamber. The bed was adapted from a royal canopy of state of George II, given to the 2nd Earl of Buckinghamshire as Lord of the Bedchamber after the King's death in 1760.

Many of the state beds to be seen at National Trust houses come from royal palaces and were either given as presents or acquired as perquisites, benefits of the job enjoyed by household officers and ambassadors. 'Perks' provided Knole in Kent with its unrivalled collection of seventeenth-century upholstered furniture. The bed now in the Spangle Bedroom was probably acquired in the 1620s by Lionel Cranfield, Earl of Middlesex when he was Master of the Great Wardrobe to James I. Although the bed was later altered, the hangings of crimson and white sewn with thousands of tiny sequins to shimmer in the light date from the early seventeenth century.

Two sumptuous state beds from Whitehall Palace were given to Lionel's grandson, Charles Sackville, 6th Earl of Dorset, in his role as Lord Chamberlain. In 1672 Jean Peyraud, upholsterer to Louis XIV, came to London to make six beds for Charles II. He not only provided the hangings but encased the woodwork of the bedsteads in fabric creating a rich plasticity. One of Peyraud's creations, now in the King's Bedroom at Knole (p.40), was made for the marriage of Charles II's brother, James, Duke of York, to Mary of Modena in 1673. Its headboard is decorated with a ducal coronet and cap of red velvet in stumpwork. The hangings are cloth of gold backed by cherry coloured satin, with crimson and white ostrich feathers as a final flourish on the tops of the bedposts.

The third state bed at Knole, of blue-green Genoa velvet, was the work of Jean Poictevin and Thomas Roberts, dating from 1688. Again it was made for James, but now he was king, having succeeded his brother three years earlier. Hardly had he laid his crowned head on the pillows, however, when James II was forced to flee the country, giving way to his daughter Mary and her husband, William of Orange. They were familiar with this style of bed, for many Huguenots had worked at the Dutch court, driven out of France through religious persecution. Foremost amongst these was Daniel Marot, who described himself as architect and decorator to William and Mary. We only have drawings of Marot's exuberant concoctions for state beds, but his style is reflected in the work of Francis Lapierre. A canopy from the state bed he made for William Cavendish, lst Duke of Devonshire, looms out in the Long Gallery at Hardwick. Another, more complete bed in the Marot/Lapierre style can be seen at Dyrham Park near Bath, the home of William III's Secretary for War, William Blaythwayt.

The title of this book is taken from the diary of Samuel Pepys, where the phrase so often finishes off his daily record. Pepys kept his diary from 1660 until 1669 when failing eyesight made it impossible for him to continue. Unlike many diarists, who record only the great events of their time, Pepys talks of more mundane occurrences, providing an unrivalled insight into seventeenth-century domestic life, including the intimacies of his bedchamber.

Pepys lived in Seething Lane in the City of London with his wife Elizabeth and a household of four servants. On 11 October 1663 he records 'bringing the green bed into our chamber, which is handsomer than the red one, though not of the colour of our hangings'. To overcome this decorating solecism he put green covers on the chairs. As a middle-ranking civil servant in the Admiralty, Pepys would not have had the fine satins and velvets of the state beds at Knole. His bed furnishings would have been of wool, possibly decorated with embroidery. Examples of this type of work, dating from the later seventeenth century, can be seen in the bedrooms at Cotehele in Cornwall.

Pepys shared his bedchamber with his wife, but it is clear from his diaries that servants might sleep there too. On 13 November 1661 he records 'this night begin to lie in the little green chamber where the maids lie; but we could not a great while get Nell to lie there because I lie there and my wife; but at last, when she saw she must be there or sit up, she with much ado came to bed.' Maybe Nell knew of Pepys' reputation with the ladies.

Apart from the bed with its curtains, Pepys had a chest of drawers, purchased in July 1661, for storing clothes. His wife would have had a dressing table, possibly like the one shown opposite, with a mirror in a dressing box, flanked by candlesticks. Pepys was always fascinated by the latest ideas and records a visit to the instrument maker, Ralph Greatorex, in October 1660, when 'he did show me the manner of the lamp glasses, which carry the light a great way. Good to read in bed by, and I intend to have one of them.' He was also taken by the idea of 'counterfeit windows' of reflecting glass, and considered having one installed in his closet adjoining the bedchamber to improve the light.

Pepys also frequently mentions taking a drink of posset before going to bed. This was made from a mixture of fortified wine with spices and cream – Pepys said the wine made him lusty, the sugar kind – and could be warmed up in a special pot by the bedroom fire. And so to bed.

After the Restoration, fashionable men and women sat for their portraits wearing nightgowns. Nightgown in this context was not what they wore in bed, but informal robes and dresses worn in the privacy of their own homes. The bedchamber was still a room used for reception of visitors, where the host would wear his night or dressing gown, and the hostess her loose 'undress', a silk robe opening down the front worn with flowing smock sleeves, as immortalised in Sir Peter Lely's portraits of beauties at the court of Charles II.

In the seventeenth century the nightgown could be purchased with matching slippers and 'toylett', a piece of silk for use as a covering for a bedroom table, on which would be placed brushes and combs. Later the term transferred from the cloth to the objects themselves. A fine toilet set, including nightgown and slippers, dating from the early years of the eighteenth century, is on show at Ham House in Surrey.

Pepys records wearing a dressing gown while going through his naval accounts with a colleague, and chose to have his portrait painted in an Indian gown. This was probably not Indian, but refers to its oriental appearance, for the portrait, now in the National Portrait Gallery, shows a light robe cut like a kimono with no collar or shoulder seams. The idea that the exotic is appropriate for the bedroom was just as familiar to Bess of Hardwick, who furnished her beds with Indian cottons. In Sackville's portrait he acknowledges the exotic by wearing a Turkish style turban. This was the period when men began to shave their heads and wear periwigs, so a turban would not only provide relief from the scratchy wig, but also keep the head warm. Pepys went through agonies of indecision as to whether he should shave off his hair, and finally decided in the cause of hygiene to do so in 1663.

For actual wear in bed, Pepys would have worn a nightshirt, probably of fine linen, and a nightcap. His wife would have worn a similar nightgown, with a frilled cap and possibly cross cloths (see p.46) over her forehead. This fashion continued throughout the eighteenth and nineteenth centuries. Some authors link the development of attractive nightwear for ladies with the introduction of birth control. Whatever the cause, brides assembling their trousseaux in the 1890s chose frothy confections with gathered waists, puffed shoulder sleeves and lavish trimmings of baby-ribbons, preferably in pastel shades. Pyjamas, Indian in origin, were worn by men from the end of the nineteenth century, and by women after the First World War.

The royal arrangement of bedchamber and closets was reproduced by courtiers in their houses, where they often created small private apartments on the ground floor, generally at the corner of the building, at the end of an enfilade of state apartments. A little closet adjoining the bedchamber would house the close stool or chamber pot, and there would often be a backstair so that servants could discreetly empty the contents. The apartment would be completed by a closet or cabinet which often served as a dressing room, as at Knole where the King's Closet is hung with green mohair stamped to look like watered silk, combining warmth with elegance. The closet or cabinet was often the place where the head of the household could work — William III conducted his dealings with his ministers in his cabinet, hence the modern use of the term for the chief ministers of a government.

Ham House was refurnished in the 1670s in very opulent style by the Duke and Duchess of Lauderdale, leading members of the Stuart court. Their private apartments are on the ground floor, on either side of the Marble Dining Room. After dressing in his closet, the Duke would turn to one of his walnut writing cabinets to work on his papers. The Duchess's Closet was furnished in the fashionable oriental style, with lacquered furniture. Here she could take tea with her friends, heating the water in a silver tea kettle, carefully apportioning the tea from a lockable caddy as this was a rare and expensive commodity, and drinking from tiny, blue and white handleless cups imported from China. The Duchess, like Queen Mary, collected oriental porcelain, arranging her pots and vases over the mantelpiece in the corner of her closet. The Duchess of Somerset adopted this practice at Petworth, and similar arrangements can be seen at Beningbrough Hall in Yorkshire.

On the upper floor at Ham, occupying pride of place in the centre of the south front, was the Queen's Bedchamber, prepared in 1673 for the visit of Charles II's consort, Catherine of Braganza. Attached to the Bedchamber is the Closet, a small room, but very richly furnished, originally with alternative sets of hangings for summer and winter. For summer there was Chinese silk with painted figures, for winter and miraculously surviving, crimson and gold brocaded satin bordered with green and gold striped silk. The alcove was probably intended to contain a couch or daybed, but is now equipped with an upholstered armchair. This is one of a pair mentioned in the 1679 inventory as a sleeping chair, with an adjustable back. Away from all the ceremony and pomp of the court, Queen Catherine could retire for an afternoon nap.

The interior of the state bed at Calke, with its Chinese silk hangings in dark blue and white embroidered with animals, human figures and pagodas. Real peacock feathers, tightly rolled, were used for the knots of tree trunks and marking of butterfly wings. This bed was probably made for George I in 1715, but was given to Lady Caroline Manners when she married Sir Henry Harpur of Calke in 1734.

When the upholsterer and cabinetmaker Thomas Chippendale published *The Gentleman and Cabinetmaker's Director* in 1754, he announced on the title page 'a large collection of the most Elegant and Useful Designs of Household Furniture in the Gothic, Chinese and Modern Tastes'. Of these, perhaps the most enduring for bedrooms was the Chinese style. Was this because *chinoiserie* had the lightness and delicacy then desired for bed-chambers? Or was it, as Gervase Jackson-Stops surmises in *The English Country House: A Grand Tour*, that 'exotic fantasies may have been considered a suitable accompaniment to the world of dreams'?

For the Best Bedroom at Erddig, in North Wales, the wealthy lawyer John Meller ordered from London in 1720 a carved and gilded gesso bedstead by John Belchier in the *lit à la duchesse* style, with the tester suspended from the ceiling rather than being supported on foot posts. The hangings and coverlet, originally white but aged to a rich ivory, are of silk embroidered in the Chinese manner, known as 'Indian needlework'. Belchier was also responsible for the bedroom furniture, a scarlet japanned bureau and a set of green japanned chairs and stools. Exquisite Chinese embroidered silk hangings can also be seen on the state bed at Calke Abbey in Derbyshire. The bed, made for George I in 1715, was a gift from his grand-daughter to Lady Caroline Manners, to celebrate her marriage to Sir Henry Harpur of Calke in 1734. Shut up in boxes for many years, the exotic silk world of mandarins, dragons and pagodas glow in brilliant shades of blue, gold, red and white.

At Saltram in Devon the Parker family showed so marked a penchant for eighteenth-century *chinoiserie* that, following incendiary damage in the Second World War, the National Trust was able to create the Chinese Chippendale Bedroom from the collection of furniture in the house. The walls are hung with painted cotton hangings from the Far East, together with Chinese mirror paintings in English Rococo frames. The bed is close to one shown in Chippendale's *Director*, and may have been supplied by his workshop. Chippendale not only provided the bed for the State Bedchamber at Nostell Priory in Yorkshire, with its *en suite* furniture, including a clothes press, a dressing table and a commode with pier glass, all in Chinese style, but supervised the installation and details such as chintz curtains and blinds.

The taste for *chinoiserie* continued with the Prince Regent's extraordinary oriental extravaganza, the Brighton Pavilion. English cotton manufacturers meanwhile imitated the hand-painted oriental silks, producing not only chintzes with figurative oriental designs but also developing the floral motifs that still decorate modern bedrooms.

In 1758 the young architect, Robert Adam, returned from his studies of the monuments of classical antiquity in Italy. One of his first commissions came from Nathaniel Curzon who asked him to take over the building of his great house at Kedleston in Derbyshire, and to furnish its interior. The design for Kedleston had been set by an earlier architect, Matthew Brettingham, with a central block and pavilions joined by curving corridors. In the middle of the central block Adam placed the monumental hall and saloon, with rooms on one side devoted to the arts, and on the other to hospitality, including a State Bedchamber and its attendant Dressing Room. Dr Johnson, staying overnight in an ordinary bedroom, observed 'the grandeur is all below. The bedchambers are small, low, dark and fitter for a prison than a house of splendour'.

Neo-classicist Adam may have been, but in the State Bedchamber at Kedleston he indulged in the exotic. The posts of the state bed are of cedar wood, carved and gilded to give the effect of palm trees with writhing roots. The palm theme extends to the pier glass and candlestands, which are decorated with fronds to represent an allegory of fertility and hospitality.

Working for Robert Child the banker at Osterley Park in Middlesex, Adam moved from the exotic to the theatrical. The State Bed, based on his 1776 drawing of a 'Temple of Venus', has a bedstead of oak, beech and pine, painted and gilded. The hangings are of olive green velvet and pale green silk, embroidered in silver and other colours. The valance is decorated in panels, with the family symbol of an eagle holding an adder in its beak alternating with the marigold, the sign of Child's Bank. The whole ornate structure is topped by a dome which was intended to resemble the temple to the fertility goddess, thus celebrating the posterity of the Child family. Instead it incurred the disapproval of Horace Walpole, who considered it 'too theatric and too like a modern head-dress, for round the outside of the dome are festoons of artificial flowers. What would Vitruvius think of a dome decorated by a milliner?' Indeed there is a similarity between the dome and Adam's design for a canopied box for George III at the Italian Theatre in Haymarket.

Around the bed at Osterley are three narrow strips of carpet, designed by Robert Adam and picking out the marigold motif. This is a rare survival of a bed carpet, an eighteenth-century descendant of the fledges mentioned in the 1601 inventory of Bess of Hardwick, pieces of woollen fabric laid round the bed to protect bare feet from cold wooden flooring or rush matting.

Zoffany's painting depicts the actress Mrs Cibber learning her lines in her bedchamber, standing by her dressing table fashioned in the rococo style, possibly copied from Thomas Chippendale's highly influential *Director* (p.22). Festoons of muslin billow down from the top of the mirror, and fringed drapes hang over the recess under the central drawer. On the table, Mrs Cibber's playbook rests amid her toilet set, jars of pommade and creams. A lady preparing her face, her hair and her dress for the social round would be assisted by her lady's maid, a man by his valet.

The bedchamber itself would have been cleaned and tidied by the chambermaid. A wonderfully anarchic picture of this maid and her duties is painted by Jonathan Swift in his *Directions to Servants* published in 1745:

> Your particular Province is your Lady's Chamber, where you make the Bed, and put Things in order; and if you live in the Country, you take Care of Rooms where Ladies lie who come into the House, which brings in all the Vails [tips] that fall to your share. Your usual Lover, as I take it, is the Coachman; but if you are under Twenty, and tolerably handsome, perhaps a Footman may cast his eyes on you.

Swift goes on to suggest the chambermaid should empty her mistress's chamber pot out of the window to avoid other servants realising that 'fine Ladies have occasion for such Utensils', and that while making the bed in hot weather, she should use the sheet to mop her brow.

In more serious vein are the instructions produced in 1776 by Susannah Whatman for her household at Turkey Court in Kent. She warns the chambermaid to keep the sun out of bedrooms and dressing rooms to avoid spoiling the carpet, chairs and mahogany clothes presses. She suggests that paper should be kept on the top of the testers of beds to catch dust, and that these be replaced twice a year.

When the household was away, the chambermaid would encase four poster beds with case curtains to protect the fine fabrics not only from light, but also dust. The state bed at Dyrham Park, for instance (p.14), had extra curtains of worsted paragon – a light wool – hung on separate rods to protect the silks and velvets, and these have been reconstructed. Today, when the National Trust puts its houses to bed at the end of the visiting season, beds and other pieces of furniture are similarly encased.

When George Hammond Lucy married Mary Elizabeth Williams in December 1823, he had recently inherited Charlecote Park, a picturesque Tudor mansion in Warwickshire with Shakespearean connections and much dilapidation. The young couple worked hard to return the house to its former glory, buying furniture that they thought dated from the sixteenth century. One such piece was the 'Lancaster State Bed' bought from William Beckford through a Bath auctioneer and cabinetmaker in 1837. Visitors to Beckford's wildly extravagant Fonthill Abbey in Wiltshire had enjoyed the privilege of sleeping in the bed under Henry VII's purple silk quilt. Now the bedstead, not in fact Tudor at all, but fashioned from a seventeenth-century East Indian settee in ebony, was installed in the Ebony Bedroom at Charlecote, along with its paliasse, two mattresses, a feather bed bolster, two pillows and the silk quilt.

Historic recreations, if possible with romantic associations, were the order of the day. At Hardwick Hall, the Dukes of Devonshire were evoking the shade not only of their great ancestress, Bess of Hardwick, but also of Mary Queen of Scots, who spent her captivity in the custody of Bess's fourth husband, the Earl of Shrewsbury. Mary never stayed at Hardwick, which was built after her execution, but no matter: a room was furnished in the appropriate style and a touch of authenticity provided by bringing a carved panel of her coat of arms from Chatsworth. It was then known as the Mary Queen of Scots Bedchamber.

Many apparently late medieval or Elizabethan bedchambers in National Trust houses are in fact recreations of the eighteenth and nineteenth centuries. Furniture makers were often called upon to rework old carved cabinets to make them into venerable beds. Wightwick Manor in the West Midlands was built in the 1880s in the 'Old English' style and contains a superb collection of William Morris fabrics and furnishings. The Acanthus Bedroom contains a nineteenth-century Italian bed incorporating seventeenth-century marquetry and ivory panels. The Honeysuckle Room, the most intensely 'Morris' interior in the house, has an eighteenth-century Gothick four poster bed with bed-hangings designed and embroidered by May Morris, William's daughter, and a Jacobean-style bedcover.

But not even Morris and his circle went to the lengths of Charles Paget Wade at Snowshill. Wade, a fervent believer in the importance of preserving objects made by craftsmen, so filled his Gloucestershire manor with collections that he was obliged to move out and take up residence in the priest's house next door. There he recreated a late medieval world, cooking at an enormous open hearth and sleeping in a cupboard bed until his departure from Snowshill in 1956.

The bedroom, having wandered over the centuries from the ground floor to upper levels according to the dictates of fashion and status, was almost always located upstairs in the nineteenth century. Gone was the idea of the grand vista of state apartments: the aim now was for privacy, with bedrooms leading off corridors. At Blickling a whole series of bedrooms, known as the Lothian Row, were provided on the top floor. Each room was assigned a letter of the family name. At Tatton Park in Cheshire, reorganised in 1811, there were no fewer than twenty-four bedrooms, including six guest suites. This ever-increasing number of bedrooms was required to accommodate guests on their country house weekend visits, such a feature of the nineteenth century.

One of the major suppliers of nineteenth-century bedroom furniture was Gillows. First established in the 1730s in Lancaster, within easy reach of the Liverpool import trade in exotic woods such as mahogany, the firm prospered, opening up a combined factory and retail outlet in London's Oxford Street. Many National Trust houses have Gillow pieces, but perhaps the most complete is the bedroom furniture at Tatton: each bedroom was provided with a four poster, bed-steps – essential with the heavily stuffed mattresses and feather bolsters of the period – a Grecian couch, 'curricle' chairs, fire-screen, cheval glass, pot cupboard and bidet.

In time Regency restraint gave way to Victorian excess. Not only did the number of items deemed suitable for a bedroom proliferate, but they grew ever more massive and complex. Von Falke, writing *Art in the House* in 1879 announced complacently 'from the early part of the present century, until the impetus given to Art by the Great Exhibition had had time to take effect, the general taste in furnishing houses of all but a very few persons was at about its worst'.

In the Silk Bedroom at Tatton the posts of the bed were cut down and the tester cut back to accord with the fashion for half-testers. A fine half-tester bed in South American black walnut can be seen in the Owl Bedroom at Cragside in Northumberland. Designed by the architect Norman Shaw for the visit of the Prince and Princess of Wales in 1884, it has owls standing on guard at its feet.

Bedroom styles proliferated alongside the number of items: 'Adam', 'Sheraton', 'Hepplewhite' jostled with Gothic, Rococo and Baroque. At Penrhyn Castle, Thomas Hopper designed 'Norman' bedroom furniture for the extraordinary Norman keep that he built for the Douglas-Pennant family. And at Cragside in the White Bedroom can be seen the 'Quaint' style, a reflection of the cottage style introduced by the Arts & Crafts Movement.

The Victorian bedroom was no longer accompanied by closets and cabinets. Instead, a lady would retire to her boudoir to relax and entertain friends. At Lanhydrock Lady Robartes' boudoir is a very feminine room, furnished with small tub chairs, and filled with portraits of her children. A severe fire at Lanhydrock in 1881 gave Lord Robartes the opportunity to plan the reconstruction of his house in the most up to date manner, including careful segregation of public and private, master and servant, male and female. Balancing Lady Robartes' Boudoir, therefore was Lord Robartes' Dressing Room, where he could not only dress but bathe too.

Although fitted bathrooms with hot and cold water were introduced into country houses from the 1820s, many owners preferred the luxury of taking their bath in front of a fire in their bedroom or dressing room. Indeed, Lady Fry writing in the 1920s dismissed bathrooms as 'only for servants', and it was these servants who would haul the hot water up the stairs from the kitchen quarters. When Lord Robartes rebuilt Lanhydrock, he installed only three bathrooms.

Baths came in a variety of forms. One of the most ingenious is a slipper bath in the Silk Dressing Room at Tatton Park. Shaped like a boot, it has a firebox at the foot to keep the water hot, and a flue to remove the smoke up the chimney. For washing the face and hands, basins and ewers were provided on stands: these were often triangular in shape to fit into the corner of a dressing room. By the 1830s marble tops were common, with sets of dishes for washing, known as toiletries. The term that had originated in the seventeenth century as a cloth for the bedroom table (p.18) had transmogrified first to the dressing table set of combs and brushes, and now to the tooth-glass, sponge bowl, water bottle, bowl and ewer.

To make the transition from warm bath to bed comfortable, it was vital that the sheets had been suitably warmed. Probably the oldest device was an available person: in her diary, kept in the seventeenth century, Lady Anne Clifford describes a servant warming a bed for his master. A hot stone or brick from the fire, wrapped in a blanket would serve, but by the end of the Middle Ages warming pans were used on the beds of the wealthy and privileged. Henry VIII's was made in copper gilt, while Elizabeth I's was so finely decorated that it merited inclusion in her list of jewels and plate. But by the nineteenth century the ubiquitous bedwarmer was the stoneware bottle. The great Liberal Prime Minister, William Gladstone, doubled up the use of his: he would fill it with hot tea, which he drank when he awoke.

The mid-nineteenth century saw the introduction of the brass and iron bedstead. This was not a new idea – the Romans used metal bedsteads which they could fold and carry easily – but for some unknown reason the fashion never caught on until the 1851 Great Exhibition. A 'French' double bed of brass from Birmingham selling at the rate of 400 per week in 1849, shot up to 5,000 after it featured at the Exhibition in Hyde Park.

These bedsteads could be very grand: at Penrhyn Castle in North Wales an ornate brass bed prepared for the visit of the Prince of Wales in 1894 can be seen in one of the Keep Bedrooms. For the servants' rooms, plain single beds were considered more appropriate, as at Lanhydrock in Cornwall. Initially the mattress was laid on stout metal lathes, but the day of the spiral spring was at last approaching. Although carriage makers had been using sprung suspension for two hundred years, bed manufacturers could not follow suit until they found a way of keeping the springs in place.

The metal bedstead was also the enemy of the bed bug. Sleepers were susceptible to the unwelcome attentions of lice, fleas and bugs, but of the three the bug seems to have been the most hated. *Cimex lectularius*, a blood-sucking insect, first appeared in Britain in the sixteenth century. It particularly enjoyed wooden bedsteads, flattening itself to creep into narrow spaces where it lay in wait to bite the unwary.

Jane, wife of the writer and historian Thomas Carlyle, had a particular aversion to bugs, which she often allied with an obsession about the habits of her servants. On returning one day to their London home in Cheyne Walk in Chelsea, Carlyle complained that bugs had got into his bed. Jane duly checked:

> I proceed to toss over his pillows and blankets with a certain sense of injury! But, on a sudden, I paused in my operations; I stooped to look at something the size of a pin point; a cold shudder ran over me; as sure as I lived it was an infant bug! And, oh heaven, that bug, little as it was, must have parents – grandfathers and grandmothers, perhaps!

The maidservant pointed out that bugs were inevitable in London and that in light of the implied criticism of her cleaning habits she intended to give notice, so that Jane Carlyle bemoaned returning to 'a house full of bugs and evil passions'.

Bugs doubtless flourished because mattresses were often filled with dirty feathers and rubbish. So although manufacturers of metal bedsteads proclaimed that their products were responsible for the diminution of the ubiquitous nuisance, thanks must also be laid at the feet of the cotton coverings which replaced wool for mattresses and bolsters. The washable cotton enabled the bugs to be exterminated by boiling.

Almost all the beds and bedrooms described in this book have belonged to the wealthy: this is inevitable given that the National Trust looks after large country houses, and that luxurious beds are the most likely to survive. But what of the poor and their sleeping quarters?

For most of the population of Britain, right up to the twentieth century, quarters were cramped and privacy rare. In country cottages or town dwellings, the limited space available would double up for living during the day and sleeping at night. One neat solution was to keep the bed in a cupboard, and examples of this arrangement survive in the Tenement House in Glasgow, looked after by the National Trust for Scotland. Children would share one bed, while the drawers of chests would provide a makeshift cradle for babies. In the Apprentice House at Styal Mill in Cheshire, visitors can see how the pauper apprentices working at the cotton mill slept two or three to a box bed in the dormitories.

Until the mid-seventeenth century, servants in large households often slept on the floor of their master or mistress's chamber, or they took their ease where they might in the great hall, kitchens and corridors of the house. With the Restoration came the separation of the family from their servants. The senior servants would have their own bedrooms, often close to their domains, so that the butler slept near his pantry, the lady's maid within summoning distance of her mistress, and the cook in her closet above or adjoining the kitchen. Other ranks would be accommodated in dormitories or bedrooms in the attics.

Little early furniture for servants' bedrooms survives, but an inventory drawn up for The Vyne in Hampshire in 1754 lists the furniture in the cook's room: two half canopy bedsteads with feather bed, bolsters, blankets and coverlets; a wainscot table, two chairs; firedogs, tongs, a shovel, brush and bellows. The value of these pieces came to £3 5s 0d, compared to the master bedchamber, where the furnishings were estimated at £96 17s 6d.

At Lanhydrock in Cornwall the servants were lodged in the attics, men and women strictly segregated, with access by separate staircases. Some of these bedrooms are on show, with their brass and iron bedsteads and pine furniture. For servants who had to travel with their masters and mistresses, a kist or mobile lodging box was an essential piece of bedroom furniture.

The Small Bedroom at
2 Willow Road, Hampstead,
showing Erno Goldfinger's clever
use of space. On the left is
a bed that can be tipped up to
stow away, on the right
a washbasin in
a cupboard.

By the beginning of the twentieth century, as far as bedroom style was concerned, anything went; there was no prevailing fashion.

At Kingston Lacy in Dorset, the White Bedroom was redecorated in 1897. It is a delightfully light room, with white painted furniture, a delicate striped wallpaper and floral chintz for the hangings. The bed has a frothy, rococo style headboard.

Hill House in Helensburgh, to the west of Glasgow, was built in 1902 by Charles Rennie Mackintosh for Walter Blackie, the publisher. The Main Bedroom is decorated in white, like the bedroom at Kingston Lacy, but there the similarity ends. Mackintosh was determined to get away from the pastiches that were in vogue, and find a style that accommodated the limitations of materials and methods of the craftsmen. The result is dramatically stark; a plain white bed decorated with organic motifs so typical of Mackintosh's work. The furniture is similarly plain: the famous long back chairs, a little dressing table, a cheval mirror, and built-in wardrobes.

From 1923, 7 Blyth Grove in Worksop, Nottinghamshire, was the home of William Straw, a moderately well-to-do grocer. When William died suddenly in 1932 the blow was so devastating that his family allowed nothing to change from that day forward, and the semi-detached house was frozen in time. The master bedroom is furnished in the heavy style of the period, with the brass bedstead dominating the small room, a dressing table of yew with attached looking-glass and lace runner, lace curtains at the window and a towel rail in front of the tiled fireplace. Susannah Whatman would no doubt have approved of the newspaper laid on the bed to keep off the dust (see p.26), but might have been surprised by the idea of storing various articles of clothing between the blankets to keep them flat.

In Hampstead, North London, 2 Willow Road also has bedrooms furnished in the 1930s, but again the contrast is startling. The house was completed in 1939 by the Modernist designer Erno Goldfinger. The bedrooms on the second floor are not large, but have a feeling of space through clever use of built-in furniture. In the Main Bedroom the wardrobes are fitted with wooden trays, their dimensions carefully calculated to store particular articles of dress. A dressing table for Mrs Goldfinger is built into the adjoining bathroom. The simple bed is set low, for Goldfinger believed that higher civilisations, such as the Japanese, slept closer to the ground. Like the bedroom at Hill House, the decoration is white. The desire to make the best of the space extends to the Spare Bedroom, with its tip-up bed and washbasin in a cupboard, and to the Nursery, where the nanny's bed could be folded away into a cupboard during the day.

The Marriage Bed

The bed made for the marriage of James, Duke of York and Mary of Modena in 1673. It was probably made by Louis XIV's upholsterer, Jean Peyrard, in gold and silver brocade lined with cherry satin. It now stands in the King's Room at Knole, together with its en suite furniture, and the magnificent silver pieces acquired by Charles Sackville.

When William, Prince of Orange, married Mary Stuart in 1642, court ritual, as ever, was brought into play. William was fourteen, and Mary ten, so the marriage was solemnised but not consummated. Nevertheless the Princess was duly placed in a state bed of blue velvet. Her young groom, clad in night robe and slippers, was brought to her by her father, King Charles I. They lay together for three-quarters of an hour, watched by 'all the great lords and ladies of England, the four Ambassadors of the United States [of Holland], and the distinguished personages who attended him'.

One of the great lords present at the ceremony was the bride's brother, James, Duke of York, but no such formality accompanied his second marriage. His bride, Mary of Modena, arrived at Dover on 21 November 1673, and according to his diary was wedded and bedded that night. Perhaps word had reached him of how the eighteen-year-old Italian princess screamed for two days and nights when she learnt that she was to wed a forty-year-old English duke rather than become a bride of Christ in a convent. The state bed made to the celebrate this marriage is now in the King's Room at Knole (p.14), together with the matching chairs and stools, appropriately carved with *amorini* holding bows and quivers and billing doves.

The colour green was associated with the goddess of love, Venus, and was therefore often used for marriage beds. At Houghton Hall in Norfolk, the magnificent early eighteenth-century state bed has a headboard in the form of a scallop shell – an allusion to Venus rising from the waves.

The bedding of ordinary married mortals followed a more relaxed style. The diarist John Evelyn attending a Jewish wedding in Venice in 1644 described how the 'bed was dressed up with flowers'; violets and jasmine were recommended for English bridal beds. The bride would be escorted to the chamber by her husband's attendants; the groom, by the bridesmaids. The ballad of Arthur of Bradley, printed in 1661, describes the junketing that might ensue.

> And then did they foot it and toss it
> Till the cook had brought up the posset …
> And so all at the bedside
> Took leave of Arthur and his bride

The singing, dancing, and general horseplay would often end with 'flinging the stocking', an early version of the modern tossing of the bridal bouquet. Whoever was hit by the stocking or a garter thrown by the bride or groom, would be the next to wed.

The Childbed

In Tudor and Stuart times the bedchamber when used for childbirth was an intensely female environment. The expectant mother was supported in her labour by family, friends and by midwives, 'godly, expert and learned women' who were supposed to be licensed by the Church. Only later did their status decline, reflecting the rise of the male medical practitioner, to the point where Charles Dickens could depict Sarah Gamp as a drunken, manipulative attender of the bedside in *Martin Chuzzlewit*.

The midwife was responsible for preparing the birthroom with clean clothes and fresh bedding, including a white linen sheet to cover the bed during lying-in, and swaddling clothes and mantle for the baby. The mother could be delivered lying in bed, or sitting on a chair or a 'groaning stool', often supplied by the midwife. Above all, the birthchamber should be warm, dark and snug: a seventeenth-century manual recommended, 'you must lay the woman in a warm place, lest her mind should be distressed with too much light'. The midwife needed all the expertise and learning she could muster, for childbirth was a dangerous time for both mother and baby, whether rich or poor. Accounts of the period chronicle not only the sad losses of child after child at birth or soon after, but also the death of the mother both in labour or from a subsequent infection.

If a safe delivery was achieved, mother and baby would be bathed in warm water and anointed with oils. According to the *Expert Midwife*, published in 1637, the ointment should be concocted from the juice of rue, herb-race, myrrh, linseed, fenugreek and barley meal. The baby would then be shown to the happy father and the men waiting outside the birthchamber before being swaddled and laid in a cradle (p.46). Meanwhile the mother would remain in bed in the same dark, snug environment, for a period known as 'in the straw'. At the end of this time, usually a week or so, the mother was removed from her soiled bedding for 'upsitting'. The very detailed family accounts of the Verneys of Claydon in Oxfordshire describe how in 1647, Lady Mary took longer to recover from the birth of her son Ralph. 'Since I was brought to bed, I have never been able to sit up an hour at a time', she wrote three weeks after the birth. But a week later she was sufficiently recovered to enact the final stage of the ritual – churching – which marked the return of the mother to everyday life. Some churchmen insisted on linking childbirth with original sin, but Samuel Pepys would have none of this. In May 1662 he recorded hearing Mr Westrup praying 'that God would deliver [a mother] from the hereditary curse of childbearing, which seemed a pretty strange expression'.

Children's Bedrooms

The late nineteenth-century Night Nursery at Lanhydrock, with muslin festooned cots and iron bedsteads for the older children.

The snug, womb-like environment of the birth chamber (p.42) was likewise recommended for the new-born baby. The *Midwives Book* of 1671 advised: 'Let not the beams of the sun or moon dart upon it as it lieth in the cradle especially, but let the cradle stand in a darkish and shadowy place'. The cradle was usually made of wood with rockers to lull the baby to sleep. Hogarth's painting of Gerard Anne Edwards, now at Upton House in Warwickshire, shows an unusually elaborate cradle of wicker draped with yards of quilted fabric, but Master Edwards was heir to a substantial estate. For the first four to six weeks of life, children were wrapped in swaddling clothes, a universal practice until the early eighteenth century. The baby would be dressed in a small garment like a shirt, and bandages wound spirally the length of the body. Its physical needs were catered for with a tail clout.

Even wealthy children might not have their own bedroom. Lady Arabella Stuart had a bedstead in her grandmother's chamber (p.6), while Lady Anne Clifford, heiress to extensive estates in Cumbria and Westmorland, records in her Knole Diary that she slept on a pallet in the chamber of her aunt, Lady Warwick when she was at court. Indeed, she noted that being made to sleep in a chamber on her own was a punishment from her mother.

No nursery or children's lodgings survive from the sixteenth and seventeenth centuries, but records reveal how they were furnished. At Belton House in Lincolnshire, built by the Brownlow family in the late seventeenth century, the main nursery is described in an inventory as containing two four-poster beds, one with hangings of crimson mohair, the second curtained in grey angora. The 'little nurserie' had a bedstead with purple curtains and a cradle with feather mattress and pillows.

The heyday of the nursery came in the nineteenth century, when children were accommodated within easy reach of their mother's bedroom. This may have been due to the influence of Queen Victoria and Prince Albert, who liked to be near their many children. At Lanhydrock in Cornwall, the nursery was situated on the first floor, a self-sufficient unit consisting of a suite of rooms – scullery, night and day nurseries, Nanny's bedroom, bathroom, and a spare nursery for visiting children.

In the night nursery the Robartes children slept on metal bedsteads, advancing from the cots with their festoons of muslin lace to the rather austere beds. When they were old enough, they left the domain of the nanny and had bedrooms of their own elsewhere in the house.

The Deathbed

On 28 December 1694, Mary II died of smallpox, aged only 32, to the devastation of her husband, William III, and of the nation. The diarist Celia Fiennes described how her body lay in state first at Whitehall Palace 'in a bed of purple velvet all open …a halfe-pace [dais] railed as the manner of princes' beds are; … and at the 4 corners of the bed stood 4 of the Ladies of the Bedchamber – Countesses – with veils'. To the sublime music of Henry Purcell, composed for the occasion, the Queen's body travelled to West-minster Abbey, where it lay on a second bed, this time of black velvet fringed with silver. This scene was echoed in 1936 when the body of George V lay in state in Westminster Hall, with his four sons standing at the corners of the catafalque.

The passing of life was marked with as much solemnity as could be afforded. The seventeenth-century Verneys of Claydon kept 'Black clothe hangings 3 yardes deepe and foure and a halfe yardes longe' together with a black bed for family bereavements. Two black taffeta nightclothes with black nightcaps are also recorded, while a young Verney widow had to be excused to her visiting relatives for having a white counterpane on her bed. Beds were even painted black on occasion. The gilded furniture in the King's Bedroom at Knole, made for the marriage of James, Duke of York, and Mary of Modena (p.40), was later painted black, probably for the death of the 6th Earl of Dorset in 1706. At Townend, a yeoman farmer's house in Troutbeck, Cumbria, bodies were laid out after death in the State Bedroom. Drinking glasses, still in the room, were provided for those who attended the wake. The death bed reached heights of complexity and sentiment-ality in Victorian times. Strict codes of conduct for mourning were laid down, and mourning warehouses, such as the department store Peter Robinson, sold appropriate dress and furnishings.

In 1840 Charles Dickens began to write *The Old Curiosity Shop*, publishing two chapters each week. As he unveiled the drama of the sufferings of Little Nell, so audiences in Britain and America built themselves into a frenzy: he wrote of being 'inundated by imploring letters recommending poor little Nell to Mercy', while crowds gathered on the quayside in New York to receive the next instalment. The climax came late that year, with the most famous deathbed scene in English literature. Nell died in the country in bleak mid-winter like a little bird, with berries and leaves as her funerary furniture: 'For she was dead. There upon her little bed, she lay at rest.'

Books Consulted

National Trust and National Trust for Scotland property guidebooks
Jane Ashelford, *The Art of Dress: Clothes & Society, 1500–1914*, National Trust, 1996
Geoffrey Beard, *Upholsterers and Interior Furnishings in England*, Yale University Press, 1997
L.O.J. Boynton, 'The Bed Bug and the "Age of Elegance"', *Journal of the Furniture
    History Society*, Vol. I, 1965
David Cressy, *Birth, Marriage & Death: Ritual, Religion, and the Life-Cycle in Tudor and Stuart England*,
    Oxford University Press, 1997
Eileen Harris, *Going to Bed*, Victoria & Albert Museum, 1981
Santina Levy, *An Elizabethan Inheritance: The Hardwick Hall Textiles*, National Trust, 1998
Gervase Jackson-Stops, *The English Country House: A Grand Tour*, Weidenfeld & Nicolson, 1985
Peter Thornton, *Seventeenth-Century Interior Decoration in England, France and Holland*,
    Yale University Press, 1978
Simon Thurley, *The Royal Palaces of Tudor England*, Yale University Press, 1993
Lawrence Wright, *Warm and Snug*, Routledge, Kegan Paul, 1962

Photographs

The National Trust Photographic Library
Andreas von Einsiedel p.14, p.29, p.31, p.33, p.35, p.37, p.41, p.45, back cover
Angelo Hornak p5 (Bearsted collection), p.15
Nadia MacKenzie p.7, p.11
John Hammond p.9
John Bethell p.13
NTPL p.19
Bill Batten p.21, p.25
Mark Fiennes p.23
Charlotte Wood p.27
Dennis Gilbert p.39

The publishers also wish to thank

The National Portrait Gallery front cover
Pepys Library, Magdalene College, Cambridge p.17
Walker Art Gallery, Liverpool p.43
Tate Gallery p.47